From Passion to Profession: Achieving Career Aspirations in Social Work and Community Development

Jasper Petersen

Copyright © [2023]

Title: From Passion to Profession: Achieving Career Aspirations in Social Work and Community Development

Author: Jasper Petersen

All rights reserved. No part of this publication may be reproduced, stored in a retrieval system, or transmitted in any form or by any means, electronic, mechanical, photocopying, recording, or otherwise, without the prior written permission of the publisher or author, except in the case of brief quotations embodied in critical reviews and certain other noncommercial uses permitted by copyright law.

This book was printed and published by [Publisher's Jasper Petersen] in [2023]

ISBN:

TABLE OF CONTENTS

Chapter 1: Exploring Career Aspirations in Social Work and Community Development   07

Understanding the Importance of Career Aspirations

Defining Social Work and Community Development

The Impact of Social Work and Community Development on Society

Common Career Aspirations in the Field

Chapter 2: Identifying and Setting Career Goals   15

Evaluating Personal Interests and Passions

Understanding the Different Career Paths in Social Work and Community Development

Setting Short-term and Long-term Career Goals

Aligning Career Goals with Personal Values and Beliefs

Chapter 3: Researching and Exploring Career Options 23

Conducting In-depth Research on Potential Career Paths

Exploring Different Work Environments in the Field

Networking and Connecting with Professionals in Social Work and Community Development

Shadowing and Volunteering to Gain Hands-on Experience

Chapter 4: Developing Skills and Qualifications for Career Success 31

Identifying Essential Skills for Social Work and Community Development

Pursuing Relevant Education and Training Opportunities

Gaining Practical Experience through Internships and Field Placements

Building a Strong Professional Network

Chapter 5: Creating a Career Development Plan 39

Assessing Strengths and Areas for Improvement

Setting SMART Goals for Career Development

Creating a Timeline and Action Plan

Seeking Mentorship and Guidance for Career Growth

Chapter 6: Overcoming Challenges and Obstacles in Career Development   47

Addressing Common Challenges in Social Work and Community Development Careers

Developing Resilience and Coping Strategies

Seeking Support and Building a Supportive Network

Embracing Continuous Learning and Professional Development

Chapter 7: Navigating the Job Search Process   55

Crafting an Effective Resume and Cover Letter

Enhancing Interview Skills and Techniques

Leveraging Online Platforms and Professional Networks for Job Opportunities

Negotiating Job Offers and Making Informed Career Decisions

Chapter 8: Building a Successful Career in Social Work and Community Development   64

Excelling in the Workplace and Demonstrating Professionalism

Developing Effective Communication and Interpersonal Skills

Embracing Diversity and Cultural Sensitivity in Practice

Advocating for Social Change and Impactful Community Development

Chapter 9: Balancing Work and Personal Life 72

Recognizing the Importance of Work-Life Balance

Setting Boundaries and Prioritizing Self-Care

Managing Stress and Burnout in the Field

Finding Support Systems and Engaging in Hobbies and Activities

Chapter 10: Continuing Growth and Advancement in the Field 80

Embracing Lifelong Learning and Professional Development Opportunities

Pursuing Advanced Education and Specialization

Engaging in Research and Publications in the Field

Mentoring and Supporting the Next Generation of Social Workers and Community Development Professionals

Conclusion: Achieving Career Aspirations in Social Work and Community Development 88

Reflecting on the Journey and Accomplishments

Embracing the Rewards and Challenges of a Career in the Field

Encouragement and Inspiration for Future Career Growth and Success

Chapter 1: Exploring Career Aspirations in Social Work and Community Development

Understanding the Importance of Career Aspirations

In today's fast-paced and competitive world, it is crucial to have a clear understanding of your career aspirations and goals. Whether you are a fresh graduate, a seasoned professional, or someone contemplating a career change, having a vision for your future is essential. This subchapter aims to shed light on the significance of career aspirations and why they should not be taken lightly.

First and foremost, having career aspirations provides you with a sense of direction and purpose. It acts as a guiding force that helps you stay focused on your long-term goals and motivates you to work towards achieving them. Without a clear vision of where you want to go professionally, you may find yourself feeling lost or unfulfilled in your chosen field. By identifying your career aspirations, you create a roadmap that leads to personal and professional growth.

Furthermore, career aspirations enable you to make informed decisions about your education and training. When you have a clear idea of the career path you wish to pursue, you can choose relevant courses and acquire the necessary skills and knowledge to excel in that field. This not only increases your chances of securing a job but also ensures that you are equipped to meet the challenges and demands of your chosen profession.

Career aspirations also play a vital role in shaping your overall happiness and satisfaction in life. When you are passionate about your work and genuinely interested in what you do, it has a positive impact on your overall well-being. Research has shown that individuals who have a sense of purpose and are engaged in meaningful work experience higher levels of job satisfaction and overall life satisfaction.

Lastly, career aspirations provide you with a sense of fulfillment and accomplishment. When you set ambitious goals for yourself and work hard to achieve them, the sense of accomplishment that accompanies each milestone reached is immeasurable. This not only boosts your self-confidence but also serves as a reminder of your capabilities and potential.

In conclusion, understanding the importance of career aspirations is crucial for individuals at every stage of their professional journey. It provides direction, motivates personal growth, ensures informed decision-making, enhances happiness and satisfaction, and fosters a sense of fulfillment and accomplishment. Remember, your career aspirations are not just dreams; they are the stepping stones to a successful and fulfilling professional life.

Defining Social Work and Community Development

Social work and community development are two interconnected fields that aim to improve the well-being of individuals, families, and communities. In this subchapter, we will delve into the definitions, principles, and importance of these professions, providing insight into how they can help individuals achieve their career aspirations and goals.

Social work is a profession dedicated to enhancing the social functioning and overall quality of life for individuals, families, and communities. Social workers are compassionate professionals who work with marginalized populations, such as the elderly, children and youth, individuals with disabilities, and those struggling with mental health issues. They aim to empower individuals, advocate for their rights, and facilitate positive social changes.

Community development, on the other hand, is a collective effort to improve the living conditions and social well-being of a specific community or group of people. It involves identifying community needs, mobilizing resources, and implementing strategies to address social, economic, and environmental issues. Community development initiatives can include projects related to education, healthcare, housing, employment, and cultural preservation.

Both social work and community development share common principles and values. They emphasize the importance of social justice, equality, and human rights. Professionals in these fields believe in the inherent worth and dignity of every individual and strive to ensure that everyone has equal access to opportunities and resources.

Collaboration and community participation are key aspects of these professions, as they involve working closely with individuals, community leaders, and other stakeholders to achieve sustainable positive change.

Understanding the definitions and principles of social work and community development can greatly help individuals in their career aspirations and goals. These professions provide a platform for individuals who are passionate about helping others and making a difference in their communities. Whether it is working as a social worker in a child protection agency or leading community development projects in underserved neighborhoods, these fields offer diverse and fulfilling career options.

By pursuing a career in social work or community development, individuals can contribute to the betterment of society, tackle social injustices, and create lasting positive impact. These professions offer opportunities for personal growth, learning, and the development of essential skills such as empathy, communication, problem-solving, and leadership.

In conclusion, social work and community development are professions that are committed to enhancing the lives of individuals and communities. By understanding the definitions and principles of these fields, individuals can align their career aspirations and goals with the values of social justice, equality, and human rights. Whether it is empowering individuals through social work or driving positive change through community development, these professions offer a fulfilling path towards achieving one's career aspirations and making a meaningful contribution to society.

The Impact of Social Work and Community Development on Society

In today's complex and interconnected world, the role of social work and community development has never been more vital. This subchapter will explore the profound impact these fields have on society, shedding light on the transformative power they hold and the benefits they bring to individuals and communities alike.

Social work is a profession dedicated to improving the well-being and quality of life for individuals, families, and communities. By providing direct services, advocating for social justice, and fostering social change, social workers make a lasting impact on society. They work tirelessly to address various social issues such as poverty, homelessness, domestic violence, mental health, and substance abuse.

One of the key impacts of social work is the promotion of social justice. Social workers strive to ensure equal opportunities and access to resources for all individuals, regardless of their background or circumstances. Through their interventions, they challenge systemic inequalities, fight discrimination, and empower marginalized groups, ultimately fostering a fairer and more inclusive society.

Moreover, social workers play a crucial role in building and strengthening communities. By engaging with individuals and families, they create networks of support and foster a sense of belonging. Through community development initiatives, social workers facilitate the establishment of community organizations, promote civic engagement, and encourage grassroots movements. These efforts contribute to the overall well-being and resilience of communities, fostering a sense of unity and collective responsibility.

The impact of social work and community development extends beyond immediate beneficiaries. By addressing social problems at their root causes, these professions contribute to the prevention of future issues. For example, by providing early intervention and support to at-risk youth, social workers can help prevent juvenile delinquency and improve educational outcomes. Similarly, by addressing the underlying factors that contribute to homelessness, social workers can help break the cycle of poverty and housing instability.

In conclusion, social work and community development have a profound impact on society. Through their dedication, social workers promote social justice, empower individuals and communities, and contribute to the prevention of social issues. The transformative power of these professions is undeniable, making them essential for creating a more equitable and inclusive society for all. Whether you aspire to pursue a career in social work or community development or simply want to understand their significance, recognizing their impact is crucial in achieving your career aspirations and goals.

Common Career Aspirations in the Field

When it comes to choosing a career, it is essential to identify your passions and goals. In the field of social work and community development, there are numerous career aspirations that individuals may have. This subchapter aims to explore some of the common career aspirations in this field, providing inspiration and guidance for those seeking to make a difference in their communities.

One of the most common career aspirations is becoming a social worker. Social workers play a vital role in helping individuals, families, and communities overcome challenges and improve their overall well-being. They provide support, advocacy, and resources to vulnerable populations, such as children in need, individuals experiencing homelessness, and those struggling with mental health issues. Social workers may work in various settings, including schools, hospitals, non-profit organizations, and government agencies.

Another popular career aspiration is community development. Individuals with this goal often aspire to work towards creating positive change within their communities. They may envision themselves leading community projects, organizing events, and collaborating with local stakeholders to address pressing issues such as poverty, education inequality, or environmental sustainability. Community development professionals often work closely with community members to empower them, build partnerships, and facilitate grassroots initiatives.

For some individuals, their career aspirations lie in program management or administration roles within social work and community development organizations. These professionals are responsible for overseeing the implementation of programs, ensuring that they are aligned with the organization's mission and goals. They may also be involved in grant writing, budgeting, and staff supervision. Program managers and administrators are essential in ensuring the smooth operation and effectiveness of social work and community development initiatives.

Additionally, some individuals aspire to become researchers or educators in the field. They are passionate about studying social issues, conducting research, and disseminating knowledge to contribute to the advancement of social work and community development practices. These professionals often work in academic institutions or research organizations, dedicating their careers to generating new insights and evidence-based solutions.

Regardless of the specific career aspiration, what unites individuals in the field of social work and community development is the desire to make a positive impact on society. By pursuing these common career aspirations, individuals can contribute to building stronger, more equitable communities and improving the lives of those in need.

Whether you are a student exploring career options, a professional considering a career change, or anyone interested in making a difference, the diverse career aspirations in social work and community development offer opportunities for personal and professional growth. By aligning your passions and goals with the various paths available, you can transform your aspiration into a rewarding profession that serves both your own fulfillment and the betterment of society.

Chapter 2: Identifying and Setting Career Goals

Evaluating Personal Interests and Passions

Discovering and pursuing our passions and interests is a crucial step in achieving our career aspirations and goals. In this subchapter, we will explore the importance of evaluating our personal interests and passions and how they can guide us towards a fulfilling career in social work and community development.

Understanding our personal interests is about recognizing what truly excites and motivates us. It involves introspection and reflection to identify activities, causes, or issues that resonate deeply within us. By evaluating our personal interests, we can align our career choices with our passions, creating a sense of purpose and satisfaction in the work we do.

One way to evaluate personal interests is by considering our past experiences. Reflect on the tasks or activities that have brought you joy and fulfillment in the past. What were the common themes or underlying values in those experiences? Identifying these patterns can provide valuable insights into your true passions and help guide your career decisions.

Another approach is to explore your current interests and hobbies. What subjects or activities do you find yourself naturally drawn to outside of work? Are there any social issues or causes that you are deeply passionate about? Exploring these interests can open doors to potential career paths that align with your passions.

Furthermore, it is essential to consider the impact you want to make in the world. What social issues or challenges do you feel most strongly about? Evaluate the causes that resonate with you and consider how you can leverage your skills and interests to contribute to positive change in those areas. This evaluation will help you identify the specific field or niche within social work and community development that aligns with your aspirations.

Remember, evaluating personal interests and passions is an ongoing process. Our passions may evolve over time, and it is crucial to remain open to new experiences and opportunities. Regularly reevaluating our interests can ensure that we stay aligned with our true passions and continue to pursue a fulfilling career that makes a difference.

In conclusion, evaluating personal interests and passions is a vital step towards achieving our career aspirations in social work and community development. By understanding what truly motivates and excites us, we can align our career choices with our passions and create a meaningful impact in the world. So take the time to reflect, explore, and evaluate your personal interests, and let them guide you on the path from passion to profession.

Understanding the Different Career Paths in Social Work and Community Development

When it comes to pursuing a career in social work and community development, it is essential to recognize the diverse range of opportunities available. Whether you are passionate about helping others, creating meaningful change, or making a positive impact on society, understanding the various career paths in this field is crucial for achieving your career aspirations and goals.

One of the most common career paths in social work is becoming a social worker. Social workers play a vital role in supporting individuals, families, and communities in need. They provide counseling, advocacy, and connect people with necessary resources. Social workers can specialize in various areas such as child welfare, mental health, substance abuse, or healthcare, allowing them to focus on specific populations or issues.

Another career path to consider is community development. Community developers work closely with local communities to identify their needs and develop strategies to address them. They collaborate with stakeholders, including residents, government agencies, and nonprofit organizations, to implement programs and initiatives that promote social, economic, and environmental well-being. Community developers can work in urban planning, affordable housing, economic development, or community organizing.

For those interested in research and policy-making, a career in social work or community development can lead to opportunities in academia, think tanks, or government agencies. Researchers and policymakers contribute to the field by studying social issues, analyzing data, and developing evidence-based policies and programs. They influence decision-making processes, shape public policies, and drive systemic changes that positively impact society.

If you have an entrepreneurial spirit, you can explore starting your own nonprofit organization or social enterprise. This career path allows you to create your own vision and implement innovative solutions to social problems. By combining business acumen and a passion for social impact, you can develop sustainable initiatives that address pressing community needs while also generating revenue.

Ultimately, understanding the different career paths in social work and community development can help you align your aspirations and goals with the opportunities available. Whether you choose to become a social worker, community developer, researcher, policymaker, or social entrepreneur, each path offers unique challenges and rewards. By pursuing a career that aligns with your passion and values, you can make a lasting and meaningful difference in the lives of individuals and communities.

Setting Short-term and Long-term Career Goals

In order to achieve success in any career, it is essential to set both short-term and long-term goals. This subchapter will guide you through the process of setting effective career goals that will help you turn your passion into a profession in the fields of social work and community development.

Short-term goals are the stepping stones towards your long-term career aspirations. They are the smaller, more immediate goals that you need to accomplish along the way. These goals can include gaining relevant experience through internships or volunteer work, obtaining specific certifications or degrees, or developing certain skills and competencies. By setting short-term goals, you can ensure that you are constantly progressing towards your ultimate career goals.

Long-term goals, on the other hand, are the bigger picture aspirations that you have for your career. These goals may include reaching a specific position or level within your organization, making a significant impact in your community, or starting your own social work or community development initiative. Long-term goals provide you with a sense of direction and purpose, helping you stay motivated and focused on your career journey.

When setting both short-term and long-term career goals, it is important to make them SMART goals – specific, measurable, achievable, relevant, and time-bound. This means that your goals should be clear and well-defined, allowing you to track your progress and evaluate your success. They should also be realistic and attainable within a given timeframe, while aligning with your overall career aspirations.

To effectively set your career goals, it is crucial to reflect on your passions, interests, and values. Consider what drives you and what you envision for your future in social work and community development. By aligning your goals with your passions, you will be more motivated and committed to achieving them.

Additionally, it can be helpful to seek guidance from mentors or professionals in the field. They can provide valuable insights and advice on setting and achieving career goals, based on their own experiences and expertise.

Remember, setting short-term and long-term career goals is an ongoing process. As you progress in your career, your goals may evolve and change. It is important to regularly review and adjust your goals to ensure that they continue to align with your aspirations and passions.

By setting clear and achievable short-term and long-term career goals, you will be well on your way to turning your passion into a profession in social work and community development. Stay focused, stay motivated, and never stop pursuing your dreams.

Aligning Career Goals with Personal Values and Beliefs

Introduction:
In the journey of building a fulfilling career, it is essential to align our professional aspirations with our personal values and beliefs. Understanding the connection between our career goals and what we hold dear to us can provide direction, purpose, and a sense of fulfillment in our work. This chapter explores the significance of aligning career goals with personal values and beliefs and offers guidance on how to achieve this integration successfully.

1. Identifying Personal Values and Beliefs: To begin this process, it is crucial to reflect on our personal values and beliefs. Take time to ask yourself questions such as: What are the principles that guide my life? What are the causes or issues that I am passionate about? By understanding our core values and beliefs, we can identify the areas where our career goals should align.

2. Recognizing the Importance of Alignment: Aligning our career goals with personal values and beliefs is essential because it brings a sense of authenticity and meaning to our work. When our values and beliefs are in sync with our professional aspirations, we experience a deeper sense of purpose and motivation. This alignment also contributes to our overall happiness and well-being.

3. Evaluating Career Aspirations: Once we have identified our personal values and beliefs, it is necessary to evaluate our career aspirations. Assess whether our current or desired profession allows us to integrate these values and beliefs into

our work. Consider whether the industry or field we are in aligns with our core principles and if there are opportunities for personal growth and development.

4. Making Informed Career Choices:
If our career aspirations do not align with our personal values and beliefs, it may be necessary to reassess our choices. This could involve exploring alternative career paths or seeking opportunities within our current field that are more in line with our values. Making informed career choices ensures that our work is congruent with our authentic self.

5. Seeking Support and Guidance:
Aligning our career goals with personal values and beliefs can be a challenging task. It can be beneficial to seek support and guidance from mentors, career counselors, or like-minded individuals who have successfully integrated their values into their careers. They can provide insights, advice, and encouragement throughout the process.

Conclusion:
Aligning our career goals with our personal values and beliefs is crucial for finding fulfillment and satisfaction in our work. By reflecting on our values, evaluating our aspirations, and making informed choices, we can create a career that is not only successful but also meaningful. Remember that the journey of aligning career goals with personal values is ongoing, and periodic self-reflection is essential to ensure that we remain true to ourselves and our passions.

Chapter 3: Researching and Exploring Career Options

Conducting In-depth Research on Potential Career Paths

One of the first steps towards achieving your career aspirations and goals is to conduct in-depth research on potential career paths in the field of social work and community development. This subchapter aims to guide you through this crucial process, equipping you with the necessary tools and knowledge to make informed decisions about your future career.

Researching potential career paths involves exploring the various job opportunities, specializations, and industries within the social work and community development field. It is essential to gather information about the educational requirements, job responsibilities, salary expectations, and growth prospects associated with each potential career path.

Start your research by utilizing online resources, such as professional networking platforms, job portals, and industry-specific websites. These platforms can provide valuable insights into different career paths and connect you with professionals already working in those fields. Reach out to them for informational interviews or shadowing opportunities to gain a firsthand understanding of the realities of their work.

Additionally, consider engaging with professional organizations and attending career fairs, conferences, and workshops focused on social work and community development. These events offer opportunities to network with professionals, ask questions, and gain deeper insights into the industry.

While conducting research, it is also important to reflect on your own skills, interests, and values. Consider how they align with the different career paths you are exploring. Reflecting on your personal strengths and passions can help you identify the career paths that are most suitable for your unique aspirations.

Furthermore, do not underestimate the power of mentorship. Seek guidance from experienced professionals or professors who can provide expert advice and support throughout your career exploration process. They can offer valuable insights and help you navigate the complexities of the field.

Remember that conducting in-depth research on potential career paths is an ongoing process. As you gain more experience and knowledge, your interests and goals may evolve. Stay open-minded and adaptable to new opportunities that arise along the way.

By dedicating time and effort to researching potential career paths, you are setting yourself up for success in your journey towards achieving your career aspirations in social work and community development. So, take the initiative and start exploring the endless possibilities that await you!

Exploring Different Work Environments in the Field

In the ever-evolving field of social work and community development, it is essential to understand and explore the various work environments available to professionals. Each work environment offers unique opportunities and challenges, allowing individuals to align their career aspirations and goals with the setting that best suits their interests and skills.

One of the most common work environments in social work is the government sector. Government agencies often provide a wide range of social services, including welfare programs, child protection, and community development initiatives. Working in this sector can provide professionals with the opportunity to make a significant impact on policies and programs that directly affect individuals and communities. Additionally, government positions often offer stability and opportunities for career advancement.

Non-profit organizations are another prevalent work environment in the field. These organizations are driven by a mission to address specific social issues, such as poverty, homelessness, or mental health. Working for a non-profit allows individuals to work closely with like-minded individuals and contribute to causes they are passionate about. However, non-profit work can be demanding, often requiring individuals to wear multiple hats and work with limited resources.

For those who prefer a more clinical approach, pursuing a career in healthcare or social services can be a compelling option. Hospitals, clinics, and rehabilitation centers provide opportunities for social workers to support individuals and families facing medical challenges.

This environment allows professionals to work closely with multidisciplinary teams, including doctors, nurses, and therapists, to ensure holistic care for their clients.

Another work environment to consider is academia. Universities and research institutions offer opportunities for individuals to engage in research, teaching, and training future social work professionals. This setting allows individuals to contribute to the knowledge and development of the field, shaping the next generation of social workers.

Finally, some social workers choose to establish their own private practices. This path offers individuals the freedom to focus on specific areas of interest or expertise. Private practitioners often work with clients on an individual basis, providing counseling, therapy, or specialized services.

Ultimately, exploring different work environments in the field of social work and community development is crucial for individuals seeking to achieve their career aspirations and goals. By understanding the unique opportunities and challenges each setting brings, professionals can make informed decisions that align with their passions and skill sets. Whether it be government, non-profit, healthcare, academia, or private practice, there is a work environment for everyone in this rewarding field.

Networking and Connecting with Professionals in Social Work and Community Development

Building a successful career in social work and community development requires more than just having the necessary qualifications and skills. It also requires a strong network of professionals who can support and guide you along your journey. Networking and connecting with professionals in the field is essential for anyone who wants to achieve their career aspirations and goals in social work and community development.

Networking is not just about collecting business cards and attending events; it is about building genuine relationships with like-minded individuals who share your passion for making a difference in people's lives. By connecting with professionals in the field, you gain access to a wealth of knowledge, experience, and opportunities that can help you grow both personally and professionally.

One of the first steps in networking is identifying the individuals and organizations that align with your career aspirations and goals. Research and identify professionals who are well-respected and established in the field. Look for opportunities to attend conferences, workshops, and seminars where you can connect with these individuals. Join professional organizations and online communities where you can engage in discussions and build relationships with fellow professionals.

Once you have identified professionals you want to connect with, it is important to approach them in a respectful and genuine manner. Reach out to them through email or social media, expressing your interest in their work and your desire to connect. Offer to meet for a coffee or a virtual chat to learn more about their experiences and seek advice. Remember, networking is a two-way street, so be prepared to offer something of value in return, whether it be your skills, knowledge, or a different perspective.

Networking is not limited to professionals within your field. It is also important to connect with individuals from diverse backgrounds and disciplines. This allows you to gain fresh perspectives and broaden your understanding of social issues. Attend events or join groups that bring together professionals from various sectors, such as education, healthcare, and policy-making. Building a diverse network will not only enrich your professional life but also provide opportunities for collaboration and innovation.

In conclusion, networking and connecting with professionals in social work and community development is crucial for achieving your career aspirations and goals. By building genuine relationships and exchanging knowledge and experiences, you can enhance your skills, gain new opportunities, and make a lasting impact in the lives of those you serve. So, take the initiative and start connecting with professionals today!

Shadowing and Volunteering to Gain Hands-on Experience

As you embark on your journey towards a fulfilling career in social work and community development, it is crucial to understand the importance of gaining hands-on experience through shadowing and volunteering. This subchapter aims to shed light on the significance of these activities and how they can contribute to your career aspirations and goals.

Shadowing is a valuable opportunity that allows you to observe professionals in the field firsthand. By shadowing experienced social workers, community organizers, or community development specialists, you can gain a deeper understanding of the day-to-day responsibilities and challenges they face. This experience will provide you with a realistic perspective on the field and help you determine whether it aligns with your passions and goals.

Volunteering, on the other hand, provides a unique chance to actively engage with communities and make a meaningful impact. By dedicating your time and skills to a cause you are passionate about, you not only help those in need but also develop crucial skills and knowledge that will be invaluable in your future career. Volunteering allows you to build relationships, develop empathy, and enhance your problem-solving abilities, all of which are essential in the field of social work and community development.

Engaging in these activities can also help you build a network of professionals and mentors who can guide you along your career path. By actively participating in shadowing opportunities and volunteering initiatives, you gain exposure to professionals who can offer valuable advice, insights, and potential job opportunities. These connections can prove instrumental in achieving your career aspirations and goals.

Furthermore, shadowing and volunteering experiences provide a competitive edge in the job market. Employers in the social work and community development field highly value candidates who have practical experience and a demonstrated commitment to making a difference. By showcasing your hands-on experience, you distinguish yourself from other candidates and increase your chances of landing your dream job.

In conclusion, shadowing and volunteering are essential components of your journey towards a successful career in social work and community development. These activities offer invaluable opportunities to gain firsthand experience, develop crucial skills, build a network of professionals, and enhance your employability. Embrace these experiences, as they will undoubtedly contribute to your passion and help you achieve your career aspirations and goals.

Chapter 4: Developing Skills and Qualifications for Career Success

Identifying Essential Skills for Social Work and Community Development

In the ever-evolving field of social work and community development, it is crucial to have a clear understanding of the essential skills required to pursue a successful career. Whether you are an aspiring professional or someone seeking to enhance their current skill set, this subchapter will guide you through the essential skills needed to make a significant impact in your chosen field.

Empathy and active listening are fundamental skills for any social worker or community developer. Being able to understand and relate to the experiences and emotions of individuals and communities is essential in building trust and fostering meaningful connections. Active listening allows you to fully comprehend the needs and concerns of others, enabling you to provide appropriate support and interventions.

Effective communication skills are also vital in social work and community development. Whether you are communicating with clients, colleagues, or stakeholders, being able to clearly convey information, actively engage in conversations, and adapt your communication style to different audiences is key. Strong communication skills facilitate collaboration and ensure that everyone involved is on the same page, leading to more successful outcomes.

Critical thinking and problem-solving abilities are crucial skills for social work and community development professionals. These skills enable you to analyze complex situations, identify underlying issues, and develop innovative solutions. By thinking critically, you can address challenges and create sustainable change in individuals, communities, and systems.

Cultural competence is another essential skill in today's diverse society. Social workers and community developers must have a deep appreciation for and understanding of various cultures, beliefs, and practices. By embracing diversity and adapting your approach accordingly, you can provide inclusive and culturally sensitive services that meet the unique needs of each individual or community.

Lastly, self-care and resilience are essential skills for every social work and community development professional. The nature of this work can be emotionally and physically demanding, making it crucial to prioritize your own well-being. Developing healthy coping mechanisms, setting boundaries, and seeking support when needed will help you maintain your passion and effectiveness in the field.

In conclusion, identifying and cultivating these essential skills is crucial for anyone pursuing a career in social work and community development. By honing your empathy, active listening, communication, critical thinking, cultural competence, and self-care skills, you will be better equipped to make a lasting impact on the lives of individuals and communities. Remember, continuous learning and personal growth are essential for achieving your career aspirations and goals in this rewarding field.

Pursuing Relevant Education and Training Opportunities

In order to achieve your career aspirations and goals in social work and community development, it is crucial to pursue relevant education and training opportunities. This subchapter will guide you through the importance of continuous learning and provide practical tips on how to make the most of these opportunities.

Education and training are the cornerstones of professional growth and development. They equip you with the knowledge and skills necessary to excel in your chosen field. As the landscape of social work and community development is constantly evolving, it is essential to stay updated with the latest theories, techniques, and best practices.

One of the first steps in pursuing relevant education and training opportunities is to identify your specific career goals. Reflect on where you see yourself in the future and what skills and knowledge you need to acquire to reach those goals. This self-assessment will help you tailor your education and training endeavors to your unique needs.

There are various avenues to explore for further education and training. Consider pursuing a higher degree in social work, community development, or a related field. This will deepen your understanding of the profession and open doors to advanced career opportunities. Additionally, attending workshops, seminars, and conferences can provide valuable insights and networking opportunities.

When selecting educational programs or training courses, it is important to consider their relevance and quality. Look for programs that are accredited, recognized, and endorsed by reputable organizations in the field. This ensures that the education and training you receive meet industry standards and will be recognized by potential employers.

Furthermore, seek out mentorship and supervision opportunities. Working closely with experienced professionals in your field of interest can provide invaluable guidance and support. They can help you navigate the challenges and complexities of your chosen career path and offer insight into emerging trends and opportunities.

Lastly, remember that education and training are not limited to formal institutions. Take advantage of online resources, books, and podcasts that offer valuable insights and perspectives. Engage in self-directed learning by staying up to date with research articles and publications in your field.

By actively pursuing relevant education and training opportunities, you are investing in your future and increasing your chances of success in social work and community development. Continuous learning will not only enhance your professional skills but also contribute to your personal growth and fulfillment. So, embrace the opportunities that come your way and never stop learning.

Gaining Practical Experience through Internships and Field Placements

Internships and field placements are invaluable opportunities for individuals looking to pursue a career in social work and community development. These experiences provide hands-on training and practical knowledge that cannot be obtained solely through academic coursework. Whether you are a student seeking to gain practical experience, a career changer exploring new possibilities, or someone interested in social work and community development, internships and field placements can help you achieve your career aspirations and goals.

One of the most significant benefits of internships and field placements is the opportunity to apply theoretical knowledge to real-world situations. While classroom learning is essential, it is in the field where you truly see the impact of your work. Internships and field placements allow you to work directly with individuals and communities, applying your skills and knowledge to address their needs and challenges. This hands-on experience not only deepens your understanding but also builds confidence in your ability to make a difference.

Furthermore, internships and field placements provide a chance to network with professionals in the field. Social work and community development are highly interconnected fields, and building relationships with experienced practitioners can open doors to future employment opportunities. Mentoring relationships can offer guidance, support, and insight into the industry, helping you shape your career path.

Internships and field placements also allow you to explore different areas within social work and community development. These experiences expose you to various settings, such as schools, hospitals, non-profit organizations, and government agencies. By working in different contexts, you can discover your specific areas of interest and passion. This exploration is crucial in shaping your career aspirations and goals, as it helps you identify the areas where you can make the most impact and find fulfillment.

In addition to the practical experience gained, internships and field placements often provide academic credit and fulfill degree requirements. Many educational programs require students to complete a certain number of field hours to graduate. By successfully completing an internship or field placement, you not only acquire practical skills but also progress towards achieving your academic goals.

In conclusion, internships and field placements offer a unique opportunity for individuals looking to pursue a career in social work and community development. These experiences provide practical knowledge, networking opportunities, career exploration, and academic credit. By gaining practical experience through internships and field placements, you can bridge the gap between theory and practice, shape your career aspirations and goals, and ultimately make a meaningful difference in the lives of individuals and communities.

Building a Strong Professional Network

In today's competitive world, having a strong professional network is crucial for achieving career aspirations and goals. Whether you are a seasoned professional or just starting out in your chosen field of social work and community development, the connections you build can open doors to new opportunities, provide guidance, and help you navigate the challenges you may encounter along the way.

Networking is not just about collecting business cards or adding connections on social media platforms. It is about forging meaningful relationships with like-minded individuals who can support and inspire you on your career journey. Here are some key strategies to help you build a strong professional network:

1. Attend industry events and conferences: Make it a priority to attend conferences, workshops, and seminars related to social work and community development. These events provide an excellent opportunity to meet professionals in your field, exchange ideas, and gain insights into the latest trends and practices.

2. Join professional associations: Joining relevant professional associations can offer numerous benefits. These organizations often host networking events, provide educational resources, and offer forums for discussing industry challenges. Being an active member can help you expand your network and stay updated with industry developments.

3. Volunteer or intern: Volunteering or interning in organizations aligned with your career goals can provide valuable opportunities to meet professionals in your field. By working alongside experienced

individuals, you not only gain practical skills but also build connections that may prove invaluable in the future.

4. Utilize social media: In today's digital age, social media platforms like LinkedIn, Twitter, and Facebook can be powerful tools for networking. Create a professional online presence, engage with industry influencers, join relevant groups, and participate in discussions to expand your network beyond geographical boundaries.

5. Seek mentorship: Mentors can provide guidance, share their expertise, and offer career advice based on their own experiences. Seek out individuals who have achieved success in your field and approach them to be your mentor. Their support and insights can greatly enhance your professional growth.

Remember, building a strong professional network takes time and effort. It is about nurturing relationships, offering support to others, and being open to new opportunities. By actively investing in your network, you can accelerate your career aspirations and achieve your goals in social work and community development.

Chapter 5: Creating a Career Development Plan

Assessing Strengths and Areas for Improvement

In order to achieve our career aspirations and goals, it is essential to take a step back and analyze our strengths and areas for improvement. This process of self-assessment allows us to identify the skills and qualities that we can leverage to excel in our chosen fields, while also recognizing areas where we may need to invest more time and effort to reach our full potential.

First and foremost, it is important to acknowledge our strengths. These can be both personal and professional attributes that contribute to our success and satisfaction in our careers. When we are aware of our strengths, we can strategically align our goals and aspirations with these areas of proficiency. For example, if we possess excellent communication skills, we can focus on roles that require strong interpersonal abilities, such as counseling or advocacy. By capitalizing on our strengths, we can enhance our performance and increase our chances of achieving our career aspirations.

On the other hand, recognizing our areas for improvement is equally crucial. This allows us to identify the skills and knowledge gaps that may hinder our progress. It takes courage and self-reflection to acknowledge these areas, but doing so is the first step towards growth and development. Once we have identified our weaknesses, we can create a plan to address them. This may involve seeking additional training, enrolling in professional development courses, or seeking mentorship from experienced individuals in our field. By actively working on improving our weaknesses, we can turn them into strengths over time.

Assessing our strengths and areas for improvement is an ongoing process. As we progress in our careers, new challenges and opportunities may arise, requiring us to reevaluate our skills and adapt accordingly. Regular self-assessment allows us to stay self-aware and open to growth, ensuring that we are continuously evolving and remaining competitive in our chosen fields.

Remember, career aspirations and goals are unique to each individual. What works for one person may not necessarily work for another. By assessing our strengths and areas for improvement, we can tailor our career paths to align with our passions and interests, while also addressing any gaps that may hinder our progress. This self-reflection process is a crucial tool for anyone seeking to achieve their career aspirations in social work and community development.

Setting SMART Goals for Career Development

In order to achieve success in our careers, it is essential to set clear and achievable goals. Whether you are just starting out or looking to advance in your current profession, setting SMART goals can provide a roadmap for your career development. This subchapter will guide you through the process of setting SMART goals and help you align your career aspirations with tangible objectives.

SMART is an acronym that stands for Specific, Measurable, Achievable, Relevant, and Time-bound. When setting goals, it is crucial to ensure that they meet these criteria to increase the likelihood of success.

Specific: Start by identifying a specific goal that you want to achieve. Instead of stating a vague objective like "I want to advance in my career," be more specific, such as "I want to attain a managerial position within the next two years."

Measurable: It is important to define how you will measure the progress and success of your goals. For instance, you can measure progress by stating that you will complete a specific certification course within six months or increase your client base by 20% within a year.

Achievable: Set goals that are realistic and attainable. Consider your current skill set, resources, and time constraints. Setting unrealistic goals can lead to frustration and demotivation. Instead, focus on goals that challenge you but are within your reach.

Relevant: Ensure that your goals align with your career aspirations and overall professional growth. Ask yourself if the goal is truly relevant to your desired career path. For example, if you aspire to work in social work, a relevant goal could be completing a master's degree in social work.

Time-bound: Set a specific timeline for achieving your goals. Having a deadline creates a sense of urgency and helps you stay focused and motivated. Break down your goals into smaller milestones and assign deadlines to each of them. This will ensure you make consistent progress towards your ultimate objective.

By setting SMART goals, you will have a clear roadmap for your career development. Regularly review and revise your goals to stay on track and make adjustments as needed. Remember, goal setting is an ongoing process, and as you achieve one goal, set new ones to continue growing and advancing in your career.

Regardless of your career aspirations and goals, setting SMART goals is a valuable tool that can help you create a fulfilling and successful professional journey.

Creating a Timeline and Action Plan

One of the key steps towards achieving your career aspirations and goals in the field of social work and community development is to create a well-defined timeline and action plan. This subchapter will guide you through the process of setting clear objectives, establishing a timeline, and developing an action plan to ensure your success.

Setting clear objectives is crucial in mapping out your career path. Begin by identifying your long-term career aspirations and break them down into smaller, achievable goals. For example, if your ultimate goal is to become a program manager at a non-profit organization, you may set a short-term goal of completing a master's degree in social work or community development. By setting specific objectives, you can focus your efforts and measure your progress along the way.

Once you have established your objectives, it is important to create a timeline. A timeline provides a structure and helps you stay organized. Consider the time it will take to achieve each goal and set realistic deadlines. Remember to allow for flexibility, as unexpected opportunities or challenges may arise. By creating a timeline, you can visualize your progress and motivate yourself to stay on track.

Developing an action plan is the next step. This involves breaking down each objective into smaller, actionable steps. For instance, if your short-term goal is to complete a master's degree, your action plan may include researching and selecting suitable programs, gathering application materials, and scheduling standardized tests. By breaking down your goals into manageable tasks, you can stay focused and avoid feeling overwhelmed.

Additionally, it is important to monitor and evaluate your progress regularly. Check in on your timeline and action plan periodically to ensure you are on track. If necessary, make adjustments to your plan to accommodate any changes or obstacles that may have arisen. Regularly assessing your progress will help you stay motivated and make necessary adjustments to meet your objectives.

In conclusion, creating a timeline and action plan is essential for achieving your career aspirations and goals in social work and community development. By setting clear objectives, establishing a timeline, and developing an action plan, you can stay organized, motivated, and focused on your path towards professional success. Remember to regularly monitor and evaluate your progress, making adjustments as needed. With a well-structured plan, you can turn your passion into a fulfilling profession.

Seeking Mentorship and Guidance for Career Growth

In today's dynamic and ever-evolving professional landscape, it is essential to seek mentorship and guidance to achieve our career aspirations and goals. Whether you are a fresh graduate, a mid-career professional, or someone looking to make a career change, having a mentor can significantly enhance your personal and professional growth.

Mentorship offers a unique opportunity to learn from someone who has already achieved success in your desired field. They can provide valuable insights, guidance, and support as you navigate through the challenges and opportunities that come your way. A mentor can help you identify your strengths, weaknesses, and areas for improvement, enabling you to make informed decisions about your career path.

One of the key advantages of mentorship is the ability to gain practical knowledge and wisdom from someone who has "been there, done that." They can share their experiences, lessons learned, and best practices, helping you avoid common pitfalls and accelerate your career growth. By learning from their successes and failures, you can gain a broader perspective and make more informed choices.

Furthermore, mentors can offer a fresh perspective on your career goals and aspirations. They can challenge your assumptions, help you refine your objectives, and guide you in setting realistic and achievable targets. With their support, you can develop a clear roadmap and action plan to reach your desired destination.

Mentorship is not only about professional development; it also provides emotional and moral support. A mentor can be a trusted confidant, offering guidance during difficult times and helping you overcome challenges. They can provide encouragement, motivation, and a listening ear when you need it the most.

To find a suitable mentor, it is essential to be proactive and seek out individuals who align with your career aspirations. Attend networking events, reach out to industry professionals, and join professional organizations to expand your network. Be transparent about your goals and aspirations when approaching potential mentors, and highlight what you can bring to the table in return, such as your enthusiasm, dedication, or skills.

Remember, mentorship is a two-way street. It is not only about receiving guidance but also giving back. As you progress in your career, consider becoming a mentor yourself and paying it forward to the next generation of aspiring professionals.

In conclusion, seeking mentorship and guidance is crucial for achieving your career aspirations and goals. A mentor can provide invaluable support, knowledge, and wisdom that will propel you forward on your professional journey. So, embrace the power of mentorship and unlock your full potential.

Chapter 6: Overcoming Challenges and Obstacles in Career Development

Addressing Common Challenges in Social Work and Community Development Careers

Social work and community development careers are noble and rewarding, but they also come with their fair share of challenges. In this subchapter, we will explore some of the common hurdles that professionals in these fields often encounter, and provide guidance on how to overcome them.

One of the most prevalent challenges is burnout. Social work and community development can be emotionally and physically demanding, as you invest your time and energy into helping others. It is crucial to prioritize self-care and establish a healthy work-life balance. Engaging in activities that recharge and rejuvenate you, such as hobbies or spending time with loved ones, can help prevent burnout.

Another challenge is the limited resources available to support your work. Funding constraints and limited access to necessary tools can hinder your ability to make a significant impact. However, by seeking out partnerships with other organizations and leveraging community resources, you can maximize the impact of your work. Collaboration and networking are key in this regard, as they can open doors to new opportunities and resources.

Dealing with bureaucracy and navigating complex systems is yet another challenge in social work and community development careers.

The red tape can often delay or impede progress. It is essential to remain persistent and advocate for change. Building relationships with key stakeholders, such as government officials or community leaders, can help you navigate these systems more effectively and achieve positive outcomes for your clients and community.

Moreover, addressing the stigma associated with social work and community development is an ongoing challenge. Many people have misconceptions about the nature of these careers, often undervaluing the importance and impact of the work. Educating the public about the value of social work and community development is crucial in combating this stigma. Sharing success stories and showcasing the positive impact of these professions can help change public perception.

In conclusion, social work and community development careers come with their set of challenges, but with determination and resilience, they can be overcome. By prioritizing self-care, seeking partnerships, advocating for change, and combatting stigma, you can achieve your career aspirations and goals in these fields. Remember, your passion and dedication can make a significant difference in the lives of individuals and communities you serve.

Developing Resilience and Coping Strategies

Resilience is a fundamental quality that can greatly impact the success of your career aspirations and goals in social work and community development. It refers to the ability to bounce back from setbacks, adapt to change, and maintain a positive mindset despite the challenges you may encounter along your professional journey. In this subchapter, we will explore the importance of developing resilience and provide you with practical coping strategies to navigate through the ups and downs of your chosen path.

The field of social work and community development can be emotionally demanding and mentally draining. Dealing with the complexities of human suffering, societal injustices, and limited resources can take a toll on your well-being. However, by building resilience, you can effectively manage stress, maintain your passion, and achieve your career aspirations.

One of the key aspects of developing resilience is self-care. It is crucial to prioritize your physical and mental health, as it forms the foundation for your overall well-being. Take time to engage in activities that bring you joy, practice mindfulness and relaxation techniques, and establish a support network of like-minded individuals who can provide guidance and understanding.

Another vital element is maintaining a growth mindset. Embrace challenges as opportunities for learning and personal growth. View setbacks as temporary obstacles that can be overcome through perseverance and determination. By reframing negative experiences, you can develop a resilient mindset and remain focused on your long-term goals.

Coping strategies are essential tools in your resilience toolkit. These strategies can include setting realistic goals, practicing effective time management and organizational skills, and seeking support when needed. Building strong professional relationships and networks can help you navigate through difficult times and provide you with valuable insights and advice from experienced individuals in the field.

Remember, resilience is not about avoiding stress or challenges, but rather about developing the skills and mindset to overcome them. It is about maintaining a positive attitude, embracing adversity, and adapting to change. By cultivating resilience and utilizing coping strategies, you can achieve your career aspirations in social work and community development while maintaining your passion and well-being.

In conclusion, developing resilience and coping strategies is crucial for anyone pursuing a career in social work and community development. It helps you navigate through the challenges, maintain your passion, and achieve your long-term goals. Through self-care, a growth mindset, and practical coping strategies, you can build resilience and thrive in your chosen profession. Remember, every setback is an opportunity for growth, and every challenge is a chance to develop your resilience.

Seeking Support and Building a Supportive Network

In the journey towards achieving our career aspirations and goals, one crucial aspect that often goes unnoticed is the power of seeking support and building a supportive network. As social workers and community development professionals, we are driven by our passion to make a positive impact in the lives of others. However, this can sometimes feel overwhelming, and it is during such times that having a strong support system becomes invaluable.

Support can come in various forms, and it is important to recognize that seeking support is not a sign of weakness but rather a testament to our dedication and commitment to our chosen field. One way to seek support is by connecting with like-minded individuals who share our passion and understand the challenges we face. Joining professional associations, attending conferences, and participating in networking events are all great ways to meet individuals who can offer guidance, encouragement, and even potential job opportunities.

Additionally, seeking support can also involve reaching out to mentors or experienced professionals in our field. These individuals have already navigated the path we are on and can provide valuable insights, advice, and encouragement. Mentors can help us set realistic goals, develop strategies for success, and provide a sounding board for our ideas and concerns. Building a relationship with a mentor can be a transformative experience, as they can offer guidance and support that can propel us towards our career aspirations.

Furthermore, seeking support should not be limited to our professional networks alone. Building a supportive network that includes friends, family, and loved ones is equally important. These individuals can provide emotional support, a listening ear, and a sense of stability during challenging times. Sharing our dreams, aspirations, and setbacks with trusted loved ones can help alleviate stress and provide a fresh perspective.

In conclusion, seeking support and building a supportive network is a vital component of achieving our career aspirations and goals in social work and community development. By connecting with like-minded individuals, seeking guidance from mentors, and nurturing relationships with friends and family, we can create a support system that empowers us to overcome challenges, celebrate successes, and stay focused on our path. Remember, seeking support is not a sign of weakness but a testament to our commitment to making a positive impact in the world.

Embracing Continuous Learning and Professional Development

In today's rapidly changing world, it has become increasingly crucial for individuals to embrace continuous learning and professional development. This is even more true for those pursuing a career in social work and community development. The subchapter "Embracing Continuous Learning and Professional Development" from the book "From Passion to Profession: Achieving Career Aspirations in Social Work and Community Development" addresses individuals from all walks of life, who are eager to achieve their career aspirations and goals.

Regardless of your current stage in your career journey, the importance of continuous learning cannot be overstated. Aspire to be a lifelong learner, committed to enhancing your knowledge, skills, and competencies. By continuously seeking opportunities for growth, you will not only stay up-to-date with the latest trends and research in your field but also gain a competitive edge in your career.

Professional development is an integral part of career advancement. It involves actively seeking out experiences and resources that help you develop new skills, broaden your perspective, and deepen your understanding of the social work and community development landscape. This can be achieved through various means, such as attending workshops, conferences, and seminars, pursuing advanced degrees, participating in mentoring programs, and engaging in networking opportunities.

Moreover, embracing continuous learning and professional development enables you to adapt to the ever-evolving challenges and complexities of the social work and community development sector. By staying current with the latest theories, best practices, and innovative approaches, you will be better equipped to make a positive impact on the lives of the individuals and communities you serve.

It is also important to recognize that continuous learning and professional development are not limited to formal educational settings. Embrace informal learning opportunities, such as reading books, listening to podcasts, following influential thought leaders on social media platforms, and engaging in reflective practice. Every experience, whether big or small, can contribute to your personal and professional growth.

In conclusion, "Embracing Continuous Learning and Professional Development" is a subchapter that resonates with individuals from all walks of life who are passionate about achieving their career aspirations and goals in social work and community development. By recognizing the importance of continuous learning, seeking out professional development opportunities, and adopting a lifelong learning mindset, you will be well-equipped to navigate the dynamic and rewarding path of social work and community development.

Chapter 7: Navigating the Job Search Process

Crafting an Effective Resume and Cover Letter

When it comes to pursuing your career aspirations and goals in the field of social work and community development, one essential tool that can make all the difference is a well-crafted resume and cover letter. These two documents serve as your first impression to potential employers, showcasing your skills, experiences, and passion for the work you do. In this subchapter, we will delve into the art of crafting an effective resume and cover letter that will set you apart from the competition.

The Resume: Your resume is a snapshot of your professional journey and a powerful marketing tool. It should highlight your relevant skills, experiences, and achievements in a clear and concise manner. Start with a strong objective statement that captures your career aspirations and goals, making it evident to employers that you are a dedicated and motivated candidate.

Next, focus on your education and relevant coursework, emphasizing any specializations or certifications you have obtained. Highlight internships, volunteer work, or any hands-on experience you have gained in the field. Quantify your accomplishments to demonstrate the impact you have made in previous roles, using concrete examples and measurable outcomes.

In addition, include your technical skills, such as proficiency in software programs or languages, and highlight any professional affiliations or memberships relevant to social work and community development. Be sure to tailor your resume to the specific job you are applying for, showcasing the skills and experiences that align with the position's requirements.

The Cover Letter: Your cover letter is an opportunity to showcase your personality, passion, and enthusiasm for the field. Start with a strong opening paragraph that grabs the reader's attention and clearly states your career aspirations and goals. Use this paragraph to explain why you are passionate about social work and community development and how your skills align with the organization's mission.

In the subsequent paragraphs, highlight specific experiences and achievements that demonstrate your abilities and qualifications. Use storytelling techniques to illustrate your impact in previous roles, emphasizing the positive changes you have made in the lives of individuals or communities. Connect your experiences to the organization's values and goals, showing how you would be an asset to their team.

End your cover letter with a strong closing paragraph, reiterating your interest in the position and expressing your gratitude for the opportunity to be considered. Include your contact information and encourage the employer to reach out for further discussion.

Crafting an effective resume and cover letter requires time, effort, and attention to detail. By showcasing your skills, experiences, and passion for the field, you can increase your chances of standing out from the competition and achieving your career aspirations in social work and community development.

Enhancing Interview Skills and Techniques

Interviews are a crucial part of the job application process, and mastering the art of interviewing can significantly enhance your chances of achieving your career aspirations and goals in the field of social work and community development. Whether you are a fresh graduate looking for your first job or a seasoned professional aiming to climb the career ladder, honing your interview skills and techniques is essential for success.

Preparation is key when it comes to interviews. Start by researching the organization you are applying to. Understand its mission, values, and the specific role you are interviewing for. This knowledge will not only impress the interviewer but also help you tailor your answers to align with the organization's goals.

Practicing common interview questions is another valuable step. Consider potential questions related to your experience, skills, and knowledge in social work and community development. Reflect on your past achievements and challenges, and be ready to provide concrete examples that demonstrate your abilities. Mock interviews with friends or mentors can be immensely helpful in building your confidence and refining your responses.

Non-verbal communication plays a significant role in interviews. Maintain good eye contact, sit up straight, and use appropriate hand gestures to express yourself. Dress professionally and ensure your body language reflects confidence and enthusiasm. Remember, first impressions matter, and your body language can speak volumes about your personality and suitability for the role.

Active listening is crucial during interviews. Pay attention to the questions asked and take a moment to gather your thoughts before responding. Respond succinctly and clearly, avoiding rambling or going off-topic. Additionally, don't hesitate to ask for clarification if needed.

Demonstrating your passion for social work and community development is essential. Speak sincerely about why you are drawn to this field and share personal anecdotes that highlight your commitment. Employers appreciate candidates who possess a genuine desire to make a positive impact in the lives of others.

Finally, always remember to follow up after an interview. Sending a thank-you email or letter expressing your gratitude for the opportunity shows professionalism and can leave a lasting impression on the interviewer.

Enhancing your interview skills and techniques is an ongoing process. Continuously seeking feedback, learning from your experiences, and adapting your approach accordingly will help you refine your interviewing abilities. By mastering these skills, you will be well on your way to achieving your career aspirations and goals in the realm of social work and community development.

Leveraging Online Platforms and Professional Networks for Job Opportunities

In today's digital age, the power of online platforms and professional networks cannot be underestimated when it comes to finding job opportunities and advancing in your career. Whether you are just starting out or looking to make a career transition, harnessing the potential of these platforms can significantly enhance your chances of achieving your career aspirations and goals in the fields of social work and community development.

Online platforms, such as job boards and social media networks, have revolutionized the way job seekers connect with potential employers. These platforms offer a vast array of job listings, allowing you to explore a wide range of opportunities that align with your interests and skills. By utilizing search filters and keywords, you can narrow down your options and find positions that are tailored to your specific career goals.

One of the most effective ways to leverage online platforms is by creating a compelling and professional online presence. This includes building a strong resume and LinkedIn profile, showcasing your skills, experiences, and qualifications. Employers often use these platforms to search for potential candidates, so optimizing your online profiles can greatly increase your visibility and attract the attention of hiring managers.

Professional networks, both online and offline, are equally crucial in expanding your job opportunities. Joining industry-specific groups and associations can provide invaluable connections and insights into the social work and community development sectors. Attend networking events, conferences, and workshops to meet professionals in your field, exchange ideas, and learn about job openings that may not be advertised elsewhere.

It's essential to actively engage with your online networks by participating in discussions, sharing relevant content, and contributing to conversations. This demonstrates your expertise and passion for your field, making you a go-to resource for potential employers and colleagues. Additionally, networking is not a one-way street; remember to offer support and assistance to others in your network, as this builds trust and fosters mutually beneficial relationships.

Furthermore, online platforms and professional networks offer a wealth of resources and learning opportunities to enhance your skills and knowledge. Take advantage of webinars, online courses, and professional development programs to stay up-to-date with industry trends and best practices. By continuously expanding your skillset, you become a more attractive candidate to employers and increase your chances of achieving your career aspirations.

In conclusion, the power of online platforms and professional networks cannot be overstated when it comes to finding job opportunities and advancing in your career. By leveraging these platforms effectively, you can connect with potential employers, expand your professional network, and continuously enhance your skills. Embrace the digital landscape and take advantage of the vast opportunities it offers to achieve your career aspirations in social work and community development.

Negotiating Job Offers and Making Informed Career Decisions

In today's competitive job market, it is crucial to not only have clear career aspirations and goals but also to know how to negotiate job offers and make informed career decisions. This subchapter aims to provide you with practical strategies and insights to navigate these important aspects of your professional journey.

When it comes to negotiating job offers, it is important to remember that you have the power to advocate for yourself and ensure that your needs and expectations are met. Start by conducting thorough research on the average salary ranges and benefits for similar roles in your industry and location. This knowledge will give you a solid foundation to negotiate from.

Additionally, consider other aspects of the job offer beyond just the financial compensation. Evaluate the potential for growth and development, work-life balance, company culture, and any additional perks or benefits that are important to you. Remember that negotiation is a two-way street, and you should be prepared to discuss these aspects with your potential employer.

To make informed career decisions, it is crucial to have a clear understanding of your own career aspirations and goals. Take time to reflect on what truly motivates and fulfills you in your professional life. What are your passions, values, and long-term objectives? Knowing these will help you make decisions that align with your personal and professional desires.

Furthermore, it is essential to gather information about the different career paths and opportunities available to you. Network with professionals in your desired field, attend industry events, and seek out mentorship opportunities. The more knowledge you have about the various options, the better equipped you will be to make informed decisions about your career path.

Lastly, do not be afraid to take risks and step outside of your comfort zone. Sometimes, the most fulfilling and rewarding career decisions come from taking chances and embracing new opportunities. Trust your instincts and have confidence in your abilities, knowing that you have the power to shape your own career trajectory.

In conclusion, negotiating job offers and making informed career decisions are critical skills for achieving your career aspirations and goals. By conducting thorough research, advocating for yourself, and understanding your own desires, you can navigate the professional landscape with confidence and make choices that align with your passions and objectives. Remember, your career is a journey, and every decision you make contributes to your personal and professional growth.

Chapter 8: Building a Successful Career in Social Work and Community Development

Excelling in the Workplace and Demonstrating Professionalism

In a highly competitive job market, excelling in the workplace and demonstrating professionalism are crucial factors in achieving your career aspirations and goals in social work and community development. Whether you are just starting out in your profession or aiming for a promotion, mastering these skills will set you apart from your peers and open up new opportunities for growth and success.

Professionalism encompasses a range of qualities and behaviors that contribute to a positive work environment and promote a strong work ethic. It involves showing up on time, dressing appropriately, and adhering to the organization's policies and procedures. Being professional also means communicating effectively, respecting colleagues and clients, and maintaining confidentiality. These qualities not only reflect your personal integrity but also establish trust and credibility with your colleagues and supervisors.

To excel in the workplace, it is essential to consistently deliver high-quality work. This means taking responsibility for your tasks and meeting deadlines. Strive for excellence by going beyond the minimum requirements and seeking opportunities for professional development. Stay up-to-date with the latest research, attend relevant workshops or conferences, and seek feedback from supervisors to continuously improve your skills.

Another aspect of excelling in the workplace is collaborating with others effectively. Social work and community development are often team-driven fields, and the ability to work well with others is vital. Practice active listening, seek input from colleagues, and contribute your own ideas and expertise. Recognize and appreciate the strengths of your team members, and be willing to share credit for successes.

In addition to your technical skills, employers value employees who demonstrate leadership qualities. Take initiative, be proactive, and be willing to take on additional responsibilities when the opportunity arises. Show enthusiasm for your work and maintain a positive attitude, even in challenging situations. Employers value individuals who can inspire and motivate others, as this fosters a productive and engaged work environment.

Lastly, developing a strong professional network is essential for career growth. Attend industry events, join professional organizations, and build relationships with colleagues and mentors. Networking can provide valuable insights, opportunities for collaboration, and potential job leads.

By excelling in the workplace and demonstrating professionalism, you will not only achieve your career aspirations and goals in social work and community development but also inspire others and make a meaningful impact on the lives of the individuals and communities you serve. Remember, professionalism is not a destination but a continuous journey that requires dedication, self-reflection, and a commitment to ongoing growth and improvement.

Developing Effective Communication and Interpersonal Skills

Effective communication and interpersonal skills are crucial for success in any career, particularly in social work and community development. Whether you are just starting out in your career or looking to enhance your existing skills, this subchapter will provide valuable insights and strategies to help you develop strong communication and interpersonal skills.

One of the first steps in developing effective communication skills is to understand the importance of active listening. Listening is not just about hearing the words that are spoken; it is about truly understanding and empathizing with the speaker. By actively listening, you can establish rapport, build trust, and demonstrate your genuine interest in others. This skill is especially important when working with diverse communities and addressing sensitive issues.

Another key aspect of effective communication is the ability to clearly express your ideas and thoughts. This involves using language that is appropriate for your audience, organizing your thoughts logically, and utilizing effective non-verbal communication. By honing these skills, you can effectively convey your messages and ensure that they are understood by others.

Interpersonal skills are equally important for success in social work and community development. These skills allow you to build and maintain relationships, collaborate with others, and navigate conflicts effectively. Developing empathy, emotional intelligence, and cultural competence are essential in working with diverse populations and addressing the unique needs of individuals and communities.

In addition to these skills, it is crucial to stay updated with the latest communication technologies and platforms. Social media, online networking, and digital communication tools have become invaluable in the modern workplace. By familiarizing yourself with these tools and using them strategically, you can expand your professional network, advocate for causes, and reach a wider audience.

To develop effective communication and interpersonal skills, it is important to seek opportunities for growth and learning. This may involve attending workshops, enrolling in relevant courses, or seeking mentorship from experienced professionals. Additionally, practicing self-reflection and seeking feedback from others can help you identify areas for improvement and continue to develop these skills throughout your career.

Remember, effective communication and interpersonal skills are not just relevant to your professional life but also to your personal relationships. By continuously working on these skills, you can enhance your career aspirations and goals while also fostering meaningful connections with others in all areas of your life.

Embracing Diversity and Cultural Sensitivity in Practice

In today's increasingly interconnected world, it is essential for individuals pursuing a career in social work and community development to embrace diversity and cultivate cultural sensitivity in their practice. This subchapter aims to provide valuable insights and guidance to individuals who are passionate about their career aspirations and goals, helping them navigate the complexities of working with diverse populations.

In order to effectively serve communities, it is paramount to recognize and celebrate the rich tapestry of cultures, backgrounds, and experiences that exist within them. Embracing diversity means acknowledging and valuing differences, while fostering an inclusive environment that promotes equality and respect for all. By embracing diversity, social workers and community developers can tap into the strengths and unique perspectives of individuals from various backgrounds, ultimately leading to more impactful and sustainable change.

Cultural sensitivity is another crucial aspect of working in the field of social work and community development. It involves being aware of and understanding the cultural norms, beliefs, and practices of the communities being served. This understanding helps professionals navigate potential cultural barriers, avoid assumptions, and ensure that interventions are culturally appropriate and effective. By demonstrating cultural sensitivity, social workers and community developers can build trust and rapport with individuals and communities, fostering meaningful connections and promoting positive change.

To truly embrace diversity and cultivate cultural sensitivity, professionals must engage in continuous learning and self-reflection. This involves challenging personal biases, examining privilege, and actively seeking opportunities to expand one's knowledge and understanding of different cultures. By doing so, individuals can develop the necessary skills and competencies to engage in culturally responsive practice, which is vital for achieving career aspirations in social work and community development.

In conclusion, embracing diversity and cultural sensitivity are fundamental pillars of effective social work and community development practice. By valuing and respecting diverse perspectives, and by being culturally sensitive in our approach, we can create a more inclusive and equitable society. For those aspiring to a career in social work and community development, it is essential to continually educate themselves, challenge personal biases, and embrace diversity in order to make a lasting and meaningful impact in the lives of individuals and communities they serve.

Advocating for Social Change and Impactful Community Development

In this subchapter, we delve into the essence of advocating for social change and the significance of impactful community development. Whether you are a social work professional or someone exploring career aspirations and goals, understanding the power of advocacy and community development is crucial for creating a positive impact in society.

Advocacy serves as a catalyst for social change, enabling individuals to voice their concerns, address injustices, and fight for equal rights and opportunities. It goes beyond mere activism, as it involves actively engaging with policymakers, community leaders, and stakeholders to bring about tangible transformation. By advocating for social change, you become an agent of progress, driving the necessary shifts in policies, attitudes, and behaviors that lead to a more equitable society.

Impactful community development, on the other hand, focuses on empowering communities to become self-reliant and resilient. It involves working closely with community members to identify their needs, strengths, and aspirations, and then collaboratively designing and implementing sustainable solutions. By investing in community development, you contribute to the long-term growth and well-being of individuals and families, fostering social cohesion and a sense of belonging.

No matter your career aspirations and goals, advocating for social change and impactful community development should be an integral part of your journey. Whether you envision yourself as a social worker, community organizer, policy advocate, or any other role, understanding the dynamics of social change and community development will significantly enhance your effectiveness.

This subchapter will equip you with essential strategies, principles, and case studies to inspire and guide your path towards becoming a change-maker. You will learn how to effectively communicate your message, build alliances, and mobilize resources to support your cause. Additionally, we will explore the importance of cultural sensitivity, ethical considerations, and self-care in the pursuit of social change and community development.

By the end of this subchapter, you will have a solid foundation to pursue your career aspirations and goals in social work and community development. Whether you choose to work in a nonprofit organization, government agency, or grassroots initiative, your commitment to advocating for social change and impactful community development will be the driving force behind the transformative work you undertake.

Remember, the power to create lasting change lies within each of us. Embrace this subchapter as a guide to harnessing your passion and turning it into a profession that will make a meaningful difference in the lives of others and the communities we serve.

Chapter 9: Balancing Work and Personal Life

Recognizing the Importance of Work-Life Balance

In today's fast-paced world, achieving a work-life balance has become increasingly challenging. As we strive to succeed in our careers, it is vital to recognize the importance of maintaining a healthy equilibrium between work and personal life. This subchapter aims to shed light on the significance of work-life balance in the context of career aspirations and goals in social work and community development.

Regardless of the career path you choose, maintaining a work-life balance is essential for overall well-being and success. It allows individuals to prioritize their mental and physical health, relationships, and personal interests alongside their professional ambitions. By recognizing the significance of work-life balance early on, you can establish a foundation for a fulfilling and sustainable career.

In the field of social work and community development, where the work is often emotionally demanding and involves supporting others, maintaining a healthy work-life balance is even more critical. The nature of this profession requires individuals to invest their time and energy into helping others. However, dedicating every waking moment solely to work can lead to burnout and hinder your ability to make a lasting impact.

Achieving work-life balance is a personal journey that requires self-reflection and conscious decision-making. It involves setting clear boundaries between work and personal life, prioritizing self-care, and fostering meaningful relationships outside of work. By doing so, you can recharge and bring fresh perspectives to your career aspirations.

Additionally, work-life balance contributes to increased productivity and job satisfaction. When individuals have time to engage in activities they enjoy, such as hobbies, exercise, or spending quality time with loved ones, they return to work with renewed energy and enthusiasm. This balance enhances creativity, problem-solving abilities, and overall job performance.

To achieve work-life balance, it is essential to cultivate a supportive environment where both employers and employees acknowledge its importance. Organizations can facilitate this by promoting flexible work arrangements, encouraging time off, and providing resources for employee well-being. Similarly, individuals must advocate for their own work-life balance, communicate their needs, and seek support when necessary.

In conclusion, recognizing the importance of work-life balance is crucial for anyone seeking to achieve their career aspirations and goals, especially in social work and community development. Balancing professional ambitions with personal well-being, relationships, and interests leads to a more fulfilling and sustainable career. By prioritizing work-life balance, individuals can enhance their overall happiness, productivity, and long-term success.

Setting Boundaries and Prioritizing Self-Care

In our fast-paced and demanding world, it is crucial to set boundaries and prioritize self-care in order to achieve our career aspirations and goals in social work and community development. This subchapter aims to provide you with valuable insights and strategies to create a healthy work-life balance, enhance your well-being, and prevent burnout.

Setting boundaries is essential for maintaining a healthy professional and personal life. It involves clearly defining your limits, both in terms of workload and personal commitments. By learning to say "no" when necessary and setting realistic expectations for yourself, you will avoid spreading yourself too thin and ensure that you have the time and energy to focus on your career aspirations. Understanding your priorities and aligning them with your goals will help you make informed decisions about where to invest your time and efforts.

Prioritizing self-care is often overlooked but is crucial for long-term success in any career. Social work and community development can be emotionally and mentally demanding, making it even more important to take care of yourself. Engaging in activities that promote relaxation, such as exercise, meditation, or hobbies, can help reduce stress and maintain a positive mindset. Additionally, nurturing personal relationships and seeking support from friends, family, or mentors can provide a valuable support system.

Recognizing the signs of burnout is essential for preventing it. Burnout can manifest as physical exhaustion, emotional detachment, or a decrease in motivation. It is important to listen to your body and mind and take action when needed. This may involve seeking professional help, taking a break, or adjusting your workload. Remember, taking care of yourself is not selfish but rather a necessary step towards achieving your career aspirations.

By setting boundaries and prioritizing self-care, you are investing in your long-term success and well-being. Remember that your career aspirations are not solely about accomplishing professional goals but also about leading a fulfilling and balanced life. Taking care of yourself will enable you to show up as your best self in your work, positively impacting the lives of those you serve in social work and community development.

In conclusion, setting boundaries and prioritizing self-care are essential for achieving career aspirations and goals in social work and community development. By learning to say "no," setting realistic expectations, and engaging in self-care activities, you will create a healthy work-life balance and prevent burnout. Remember to take care of yourself, because you are the most valuable asset in your journey towards turning your passion into a profession.

Managing Stress and Burnout in the Field

Introduction:
In the fast-paced world of social work and community development, managing stress and avoiding burnout is crucial to achieving your career aspirations and goals. This subchapter will provide you with valuable insights and practical strategies to maintain your well-being while making a positive impact on others.

Understanding Stress and Burnout:
Stress is an inevitable part of any profession, especially those in the social work and community development fields. It is essential to recognize the signs of stress, such as irritability, fatigue, and decreased motivation, to prevent it from escalating into burnout. Burnout occurs when chronic stress overwhelms your ability to cope, leading to emotional exhaustion and a decline in job satisfaction.

Self-Care and Wellness:
Prioritizing self-care and maintaining your overall well-being is crucial for effectively managing stress and preventing burnout. Engage in activities that bring you joy and relaxation, such as exercise, meditation, or spending time with loved ones. Set boundaries and learn to say no when necessary to avoid overextending yourself. Remember, you cannot pour from an empty cup.

Building a Support System:
Surrounding yourself with a strong support system is vital for managing stress and burnout. Connect with colleagues, mentors, or support groups within your field who can understand and empathize

with your experiences. Sharing your challenges and seeking advice from others can provide valuable insights and help alleviate stress.

Work-Life Balance:
Maintaining a healthy work-life balance is essential for long-term success and preventing burnout. Establish clear boundaries between work and personal life and make time for activities outside of your profession. Engage in hobbies, spend time with loved ones, and take regular breaks to recharge and rejuvenate.

Seeking Professional Help:
If stress and burnout persist despite your efforts, do not hesitate to seek professional help. Consult with a therapist or counselor who specializes in work-related stress to gain a deeper understanding of your emotions and develop coping strategies tailored to your needs.

Conclusion:
Managing stress and preventing burnout is crucial for achieving your career aspirations and goals in social work and community development. By prioritizing self-care, building a support system, maintaining a healthy work-life balance, and seeking professional help when needed, you can ensure long-term success and make a lasting impact in the lives of others. Remember, taking care of yourself is not a luxury; it is a necessity.

Finding Support Systems and Engaging in Hobbies and Activities

In the journey towards achieving career aspirations and goals, it is crucial to have a strong support system and engage in hobbies and activities that foster personal growth and well-being. This subchapter explores the significance of finding support systems and the positive impact of hobbies and activities on our professional and personal lives.

Support systems play a vital role in our career development, providing us with encouragement, guidance, and emotional support. Whether it is family, friends, mentors, or colleagues, having people who believe in our aspirations and cheer us along the way can boost our confidence and motivation. These individuals can offer valuable insights, share experiences, and provide valuable networking opportunities. Cultivating these relationships requires active participation and the willingness to seek help when needed. By surrounding ourselves with positive influences, we create a foundation of support that can help us navigate challenges and celebrate achievements.

In addition to a strong support system, engaging in hobbies and activities outside of work is equally important. These activities not only provide an outlet for relaxation and stress relief but also contribute to personal growth and skill development. Pursuing hobbies allows us to explore new interests, discover hidden talents, and enhance our creativity. Engaging in activities that bring us joy and fulfillment is not only essential for our mental and emotional well-being but also has a positive impact on our professional lives. Hobbies can help us develop transferrable skills, such as problem-solving, teamwork, and time management, which are highly valued in the workplace.

Moreover, hobbies and activities can serve as a means of networking and building connections within our chosen field. Joining clubs, organizations, or volunteer groups related to our career aspirations allows us to meet like-minded individuals, exchange ideas, and gain valuable insights. These interactions can open doors to new opportunities, collaborations, and mentorship, ultimately accelerating our career growth.

In conclusion, finding support systems and engaging in hobbies and activities are integral to achieving career aspirations and goals. Building a strong support network provides the necessary encouragement and guidance, while hobbies and activities foster personal growth and skill development. By nurturing these aspects of our lives, we cultivate a well-rounded approach to our career, leading to increased satisfaction and success.

Chapter 10: Continuing Growth and Advancement in the Field

Embracing Lifelong Learning and Professional Development Opportunities

In today's rapidly changing world, it is essential to recognize the importance of lifelong learning and professional development in achieving your career aspirations and goals. Whether you are just starting your journey or have been in the social work and community development field for years, continuously seeking opportunities to expand your knowledge and skills is crucial for personal growth and professional success.

Lifelong learning refers to the ongoing process of acquiring knowledge, skills, and competencies throughout one's life. It is not limited to formal education but encompasses various informal and experiential learning opportunities. By embracing lifelong learning, you can stay ahead of emerging trends, technologies, and best practices in your field. This not only enhances your expertise but also allows you to adapt to changing circumstances and make a meaningful impact on individuals and communities you serve.

Professional development, on the other hand, focuses on improving specific skills and competencies related to your career. It involves participating in workshops, conferences, webinars, and other training programs that provide targeted learning experiences. By actively engaging in professional development, you can enhance your understanding of specialized areas within social work and community development, such as mental health, child welfare, or advocacy. This can open doors to new opportunities, expand your network, and increase your marketability in the job market.

To embrace lifelong learning and professional development opportunities, it is essential to adopt a growth mindset. This means being open to new ideas, seeking feedback, and continuously evaluating your strengths and areas for improvement. It also involves being proactive in identifying learning opportunities, whether through formal education, mentorship programs, or self-directed learning. Take advantage of online platforms, such as webinars and courses, that provide flexible learning options to fit your schedule and preferences.

Additionally, networking is a powerful tool for both lifelong learning and professional development. Engage with colleagues, join professional organizations, and attend industry events to connect with like-minded individuals who can inspire and support your career journey. Collaborating with others in your field can lead to valuable insights, shared resources, and collaborative projects that contribute to your professional growth.

Remember, embracing lifelong learning and professional development is not only beneficial to your career but also contributes to personal fulfillment and a sense of purpose. By continuously expanding your knowledge and skills, you can make a lasting impact on the lives of individuals and communities, turning your passion into a profession. So, seize every opportunity to learn, grow, and thrive in the ever-evolving field of social work and community development.

Pursuing Advanced Education and Specialization

In the ever-evolving field of social work and community development, the pursuit of advanced education and specialization is crucial for achieving career aspirations and goals. This subchapter will explore the importance of continuing education, the benefits of specialization, and how to navigate the path towards advanced learning.

Continuing education plays a significant role in keeping professionals updated with the latest research, trends, and best practices in the field. In a rapidly changing world, it is essential to stay informed and equipped with the necessary knowledge and skills to address new challenges and emerging issues. Whether you are a recent graduate or a seasoned professional, investing in your education demonstrates a commitment to personal growth and professional excellence.

Specialization within the field of social work and community development offers numerous advantages. By focusing on a specific area of expertise, professionals can deepen their understanding and skills in a particular domain. This not only enhances their ability to provide specialized services but also opens doors to new career opportunities and advancement. Whether you are passionate about mental health, child welfare, or policy advocacy, specializing allows you to become a sought-after expert in your chosen area.

However, the road to pursuing advanced education and specialization can sometimes be daunting. It is essential to have a clear plan and set realistic goals. Start by identifying your specific career aspirations and the skills or knowledge gaps you need to address. Research different educational programs, certifications, and training opportunities that align with your interests. Seek guidance from mentors or professionals in your desired field to gain insights and advice on the best path forward.

Financial considerations should also be taken into account when pursuing advanced education. Explore scholarships, grants, and financial aid options that can help alleviate the financial burden. Additionally, consider the possibility of part-time or online programs that offer flexibility while maintaining your current responsibilities.

Remember, your journey towards advanced education and specialization is unique to you. Embrace the process and view it as an opportunity for personal and professional growth. By investing in your education and specializing in your chosen field, you are not only enhancing your career prospects but also making a meaningful impact in the lives of those you serve.

In conclusion, pursuing advanced education and specialization is vital for achieving your career aspirations and goals in social work and community development. Continuing education keeps you abreast of industry developments, while specialization allows you to become an expert in your chosen field. With careful planning, financial considerations, and a commitment to personal growth, you can navigate the path towards advanced learning and make a lasting difference in the lives of others.

Engaging in Research and Publications in the Field

In today's rapidly evolving world, research and publications play a vital role in shaping the field of social work and community development. Whether you are an aspiring professional or a seasoned practitioner, actively engaging in research and publications can help you achieve your career aspirations and goals. This subchapter explores the significance of research and publications, and provides insights into how you can get involved in these areas.

Research is the cornerstone of any profession, as it allows us to gain knowledge, understand emerging trends, and develop innovative strategies to address complex social issues. Engaging in research equips you with a deeper understanding of the challenges and opportunities within your field. It also enables you to contribute to the existing body of knowledge, making a lasting impact on the lives of individuals and communities.

Publications, on the other hand, serve as a medium to disseminate research findings and share insights with a wider audience. They not only showcase your expertise but also provide a platform for networking and collaboration with like-minded professionals. By publishing your work, you establish yourself as a thought leader in your chosen field, creating opportunities for career advancement and professional recognition.

To engage in research and publications, it is crucial to stay abreast of current research trends and methodologies. Attend conferences, workshops, and seminars to learn from experts and gain exposure to cutting-edge research. Collaborate with experienced researchers and academics, as they can guide you in developing research proposals, conducting studies, and writing research papers. Seek mentorship from established professionals in your field, as they can provide invaluable guidance and support throughout the research process.

When it comes to publications, consider submitting your work to academic journals, industry magazines, or online platforms that cater to the social work and community development field. Start small by writing articles or opinion pieces for local publications or blogs. This not only helps you refine your writing skills but also builds your credibility as a writer.

Additionally, consider joining professional associations or research groups dedicated to your area of interest. These organizations often publish journals or newsletters, providing you with avenues to contribute your research and gain exposure to a wider audience.

Remember, research and publications are not limited to academic settings. Engaging in research and publications can take various forms, including program evaluations, policy analysis, or case studies. Be open to diverse opportunities and use them as stepping stones to achieve your career aspirations and goals.

In conclusion, engaging in research and publications is essential for any social work or community development professional looking to advance their career. By actively participating in research and sharing your insights through publications, you contribute to the growth of your field while simultaneously enhancing your professional reputation. Embrace the power of research and publications, and unlock new possibilities for personal and professional growth.

Mentoring and Supporting the Next Generation of Social Workers and Community Development Professionals

In today's ever-evolving world, the importance of mentorship and support for aspiring social workers and community development professionals cannot be overstated. The subchapter titled "Mentoring and Supporting the Next Generation of Social Workers and Community Development Professionals" delves into the vital role mentors play in helping individuals achieve their career aspirations in these fields.

For EVERY ONE who harbors career aspirations and goals in social work and community development, this chapter serves as a guide to finding the right mentor and building a strong support system.

Mentors are seasoned professionals who have navigated the complexities of the field and have a wealth of knowledge and experience to share. They act as catalysts, providing guidance, inspiration, and advice to their mentees. Mentors not only help individuals identify and refine their career goals but also assist in developing the necessary skills and competencies required for success.

This subchapter emphasizes the importance of seeking out mentors who align with one's career aspirations and goals. It explores various avenues for finding mentors, such as professional networks, educational institutions, and community organizations. It also highlights the significance of building meaningful relationships with mentors, fostering trust, and maintaining open lines of communication.

Furthermore, this subchapter outlines the benefits of mentorship programs and initiatives that organizations can implement to support the next generation of social workers and community development professionals. It discusses the value of mentorship in fostering personal and professional growth, enhancing job satisfaction, and reducing burnout rates.

In addition to mentors, this subchapter emphasizes the significance of building a strong support system. It encourages individuals to seek out peer networks, engage in professional development opportunities, and take advantage of resources that can aid in career advancement.

Ultimately, this subchapter aims to inspire individuals to invest in their career aspirations and goals by actively seeking out mentors and creating a robust support system. It recognizes that the path to success in social work and community development is not traveled alone, and by harnessing the power of mentorship and support, individuals can achieve their dreams and make a meaningful impact in the lives of others.

Conclusion: Achieving Career Aspirations in Social Work and Community Development

Reflecting on the Journey and Accomplishments

As we near the end of our book, "From Passion to Profession: Achieving Career Aspirations in Social Work and Community Development," it is crucial to take some time to reflect on the journey we have embarked on and the accomplishments we have achieved. This subchapter is dedicated to each and every one of you, regardless of your career aspirations and goals. Whether you are a young student just starting your professional journey or an experienced professional looking to make a change, this reflection is for you.

Throughout this book, we have explored the world of social work and community development, delving into the passion and dedication required to make a difference in the lives of others. We have discussed the importance of identifying and pursuing our career aspirations, as well as setting clear goals to guide us on our path. Now, it's time to look back at how far we have come.

Reflecting on our journey allows us to acknowledge the challenges we have faced and overcome. It gives us the opportunity to celebrate our accomplishments, big and small, and appreciate the growth we have experienced along the way. It is a reminder that even the smallest steps forward are significant and contribute to our overall progress.

Take a moment to think about the goals you set for yourself when you first started reading this book. Have you achieved any of them? How did it feel when you reached a milestone or accomplished something you once thought was out of reach? Reflecting on these moments of success can reignite your passion and motivation, reminding you why you chose this path in the first place.

However, reflection isn't just about celebrating our successes. It's also about learning from our failures and setbacks. Take the time to think about the challenges you faced and the lessons you learned from them. How have these experiences shaped you as a professional? Reflecting on our mistakes helps us grow and develop into more resilient and effective social workers and community developers.

As we reflect on our journey and accomplishments, it is important to remember that this is just the beginning. There is still much work to be done and many more goals to be achieved. Use this reflection as a stepping stone to propel yourself forward and continue making a difference in the lives of others.

In conclusion, reflecting on the journey and accomplishments is essential for personal and professional growth. It allows us to celebrate our successes, learn from our failures, and rekindle our passion for social work and community development. So, take this moment to reflect, appreciate how far you have come, and get ready to embrace the exciting challenges that lie ahead.

Embracing the Rewards and Challenges of a Career in the Field

When it comes to pursuing a career in social work and community development, it is essential to understand and appreciate both the rewards and challenges that come with it. This subchapter aims to provide insight into the various aspects of this field, catering to individuals of all backgrounds and career aspirations.

For those who have set their sights on a career in social work and community development, it is crucial to acknowledge the immense rewards that await them. One of the most fulfilling aspects of this profession is the ability to make a positive impact on the lives of others. Whether it's advocating for marginalized communities, providing essential resources, or addressing social justice issues, social workers and community developers have the power to effect meaningful change. There is no greater reward than knowing that your efforts have improved the lives of those in need.

However, it is equally important to recognize that this field also presents its fair share of challenges. Social work and community development can be emotionally demanding, as you often encounter individuals facing various hardships and traumas. It requires resilience, empathy, and the ability to navigate complex social systems. Additionally, the field is constantly evolving, with new challenges arising regularly. It is crucial to stay updated on the latest research, policies, and practices to ensure effective and impactful work.

Regardless of your specific career aspirations and goals within social work and community development, it is vital to remain adaptable and open-minded. This field offers a wide range of opportunities, from working directly with individuals and families to policy development and program management. By embracing the diversity of possibilities, you can find your niche and contribute to the greater good in a way that aligns with your passions and skills.

Furthermore, maintaining a strong support system within the field is crucial to overcoming challenges and celebrating achievements. Networking with professionals in the industry, joining professional organizations, and seeking mentorship can provide valuable guidance and support throughout your career journey.

In conclusion, the rewards of a career in social work and community development are immeasurable. The ability to make a positive impact, advocate for social justice, and improve the lives of others is an incredibly fulfilling experience. However, it is essential to acknowledge and navigate the challenges that come with it. By embracing the rewards and challenges, staying adaptable, and maintaining a strong support system, you can achieve your career aspirations and goals in social work and community development.

Encouragement and Inspiration for Future Career Growth and Success

In the journey of pursuing our career aspirations and goals, we often encounter challenges and setbacks that may leave us feeling discouraged. However, it is important to remember that success is not measured solely by the absence of obstacles but by how we overcome them. This subchapter aims to provide you with encouragement and inspiration to fuel your future career growth and success in the field of social work and community development.

Firstly, it is crucial to cultivate a strong belief in yourself and your abilities. Recognize that you possess unique talents and skills that can make a significant impact in the lives of others. Embrace your passions and let them drive you towards success. Remember, passion is the fuel that propels us forward, even during the most challenging times.

Additionally, surround yourself with positive and supportive individuals who share your aspirations. Seek out mentors and role models who can guide and inspire you along the way. Engage in networking opportunities and join professional organizations to connect with like-minded individuals who can provide valuable insights and support.

Furthermore, never underestimate the power of continuous learning and personal growth. Embrace opportunities for professional development, whether through workshops, conferences, or further education. Stay up-to-date with the latest research and trends in social work and community development, as this knowledge will empower you to make informed decisions and contribute effectively to your field.

In times of doubt or adversity, remind yourself of the impact you can make in the lives of others. Social work and community development are noble professions that offer the chance to create meaningful change. Remember the stories of individuals whose lives have been positively transformed through your work, and let these success stories fuel your determination to overcome any obstacles that come your way.

Finally, always maintain a positive mindset and never lose sight of your goals. Success rarely happens overnight, and setbacks are a natural part of any journey. Embrace these challenges as opportunities for growth and resilience, knowing that each obstacle you overcome brings you one step closer to achieving your career aspirations.

In conclusion, this subchapter emphasizes the importance of encouragement and inspiration for future career growth and success in social work and community development. Believe in yourself, surround yourself with positive influences, commit to lifelong learning, and never lose sight of your goals. With dedication and perseverance, you have the power to turn your passion into a profession that brings about positive change in the lives of countless individuals.

www.ingramcontent.com/pod-product-compliance
Lightning Source LLC
LaVergne TN
LVHW051957060526
838201LV00059B/3695